FARRAR STRAUS GIROUX BOOKS FOR YOUNG READERS
AN IMPRINT OF MACMILLAN PUBLISHING GROUP, LLC
175 FIFTH AVENUE, NEW YORK, NY 10010

PRINTED IN CHINA BY RR DONNELLEY ASIA PRINTING SOLUTIONS LTD.,
DONGGUAN CITY, GUANGDONG PROVINCE
DESIGNED BY ELLIOT KRELOFF
FIRST EDITION, 2018
1 3 5 7 9 10 8 6 4 2

MACKIDS.COM

ISBN: 978-0-374-30942-8
LIBRARY OF CONGRESS CONTROL NUMBER: 2017946973

THE WORLD OF

Disney

A WRINKLE IN TIME

THE MAKING OF THE MOVIE

BY KATE EGAN

FARRAR STRAUS GIROUX
NEW YORK

CONTENTS

INTRODUCTION

It was a dark and stormy night.

In her attic bedroom, Margaret Murry, wrapped in an old patchwork quilt, sat on the foot of her bed and watched the trees tossing in the frenzied lashing of the wind. Behind the trees clouds scudded frantically across the sky. Every few moments the moon ripped through them, creating wraithlike shadows that raced along the ground.

The house shook.

Wrapped in her quilt, Meg shook.

—Madeleine L'Engle, *A Wrinkle in Time*

In the opening lines of Madeleine L'Engle's classic novel *A Wrinkle in Time*, there's a hurricane raging just outside Meg Murry's window, and a storm in her mind as well: Why can't she get along at school, like everybody else? Why does she have to look like this, with glasses and hair that won't cooperate? Why, for that matter, does she have to be like this, impatient and intense? And where on earth is her father?

This last question nags at Meg like the persistent, cold rain. Has he left his family, as the neighbors whisper? Or has something else happened, something she can't begin to imagine?

When a mysterious stranger blows into her house, it's the first step on a fantastical journey that will bring Meg closer to her father and closer, at last, to accepting herself as she is.

Meg's adventure will take her across the universe, crossing space and time to reunite her family, summoning courage she never knew she had. Meg will experience evil and counter it with love. She will come to find strength and power in all her faults. Last but not least, Meg Murry will enter literary history, because this story of her journey—*A Wrinkle in Time*—has become a fixture in children's literature.

Generations of kids have seen their own faults and their own strengths reflected in Meg. Readers of all ages have relished her adventure and wrestled with the larger questions the novel raises about good and evil, science and philosophy, family and self.

A Wrinkle in Time is a story for all time, whether the Cold War era it came from or the unsettled world of today. And now, at last, it is a feature film brought to life by the most creative thinkers and performers of our time. Helmed by a visionary director and crew, with a star-powered cast, *Wrinkle* on the silver screen is *Wrinkle* as it's never been seen before—and yet it's every bit as adventurous, daring, and grounded in love as the novel that inspired it. Whether you are a lifelong fan of *Wrinkle* or entering its world for the first time, this film brings all of the story's light and darkness to life.

Let us travel together to explore the past, the present, and the future of *A Wrinkle in Time.*

Storm Reid as
Meg Murry

Deric McCabe as
Charles Wallace

Chris Pine as
Dr. Alex Murry

Gugu Mbatha-Raw
as Dr. Kate Murry

Levi Miller as
Calvin O'Keefe

Director Ava DuVernay

Charles Wallace and Meg, with the Murry family's faithful dog, Fortinbras

Meg's rival, Veronica Kiley, and her posse

On set in the eerie, all-alike land of Camazotz

A resident of Camazotz

The in-sync ball-bouncing of Camazotz

Meg's attic bedroom

Early concept rendering of Meg arriving on the planet of Orion

CHAPTER ONE
MADELEINE'S WORLD

"Wild nights are my glory," Mrs Whatsit said. "I just got caught in a down draft and blown off course."

"Well, at least till your socks are dry—"

"Wet socks don't bother me. I just didn't like the water squishing around in my boots. Now, don't worry about me, lamb." (Lamb was not a word one would ordinarily think of calling Mrs. Murry.) "I shall just sit down for a moment and pop on my boots and then I'll be on my way. Speaking of ways, pet, by the way, there is such a thing as a tesseract."

—Madeleine L'Engle, *A Wrinkle in Time*

Later in her life, after she had published more than sixty books and become one of the best-loved authors of her time, Madeleine L'Engle said, "Of course I'm Meg," admitting that she had modeled her most famous character on herself.

From the outside, though, her early life bore little resemblance to Meg's, and her family little resemblance to the Murrys.

The only child of older parents, Madeleine L'Engle had no brilliant younger brother like Charles Wallace and no discussion of physics at the dinner table. Her mother was an accomplished musician, her father a journalist and novelist; their New York apartment was crammed with books and bustling with artistic guests.

L'Engle herself, though, was lonely. With few children to keep her company, she turned to the company of stories and characters. Once she decided she wanted to be a writer, she never looked back. "I've been a writer ever since I could hold a pencil," she said. She wrote her first story at the age of five, and she was keeping a journal—a lifelong habit—by the time she turned eight.

L'Engle was not a distinguished student at her New York school, or at the Swiss boarding school where she was abruptly sent at age twelve while her father recovered from an illness in the Alps. It was only when she went to the Ashley Hall

School, in Charleston, South Carolina, that she began to grow into her gifts. By the time she enrolled at Smith College, she was exploring a wide range of interests in literature as well as theater and student government. All the time, she was writing.

After her college graduation, L'Engle moved to a tiny apartment in New York's Greenwich Village, where her flexible schedule as an actor allowed some time to write. She published her first two novels, *The Small Rain* and *Ilsa,* in 1945 and 1946, and she met her husband, Hugh Franklin, when she was an understudy in a production of *The Cherry Orchard.* By 1948, the young couple had a new baby and a new plan: they were leaving acting, leaving New York, and starting a brand-new life in small-town Connecticut.

L'Engle published another novel, *And Both Were Young,* the following year. It drew on her unhappy experiences in the Swiss boarding school, and Charlotte Jones Voiklis, her granddaughter, said, "The novel was an early demonstration of what turned out to be her enormous gift: storytelling as a means to navigate and transform pain and hardship."

> "It's a true hero's journey, a true epic journey, warriors fighting the darkness with light."
>
> —AVA DuVERNAY
> DIRECTOR

From the outside, this period of L'Engle's life would not have seemed painful. Together, she and Hugh ran a general store in the center of town. They were raising three small children, and L'Engle was the choir director at their church—their life was full and busy.

For L'Engle, however, it was also full of disappointment. After her early success, her career began to slow. While she did publish two more novels during these years—*Camilla* and *A Winter's Love*—she struggled to find time to write, and when she did find the time, she often wondered if her work was worthwhile. She was not paid well, not widely read, and always mindful that time spent writing was time not spent doing something else. But if she didn't write, L'Engle wondered, what would she do? Who would she be?

These were big questions that needed big answers. The minister at L'Engle's church suggested she might find guidance in the work of some German theologians, but their books put her right to sleep. Instead, she found herself reading about science.

Physicists Albert Einstein, Max Planck, and Werner Heisenberg were articulating new theories that spoke to L'Engle. As her granddaughter put it, "Their work revealed a new vision of the universe, a less conventional view not visible through our everyday experiences, which resonated with her own beliefs. In their writings she found a reverence for the beauty of the laws of the universe and for the complex and ever-unfolding understanding of it, which gave her a sense of importance and acceptance."

Madeleine L'Engle could be an imposing figure when she wanted to be!

As she read, L'Engle developed a new concept of her own place in the cosmos—and a new direction for her fiction. Jones Voiklis remembered, "My grandmother didn't have a great scientific background. Her love of science was in the metaphors they provided. She loved the idea that in opening the heart of the atom we released something we didn't have the knowledge to control. There was great creative potential—as well as great destructive potential—in that."

By 1959, L'Engle and her family were ready for another change. Hugh decided to return to his acting career in New York; before the move, the family embarked on a ten-week cross-country camping trip. It was while they were on the road that three names came to L'Engle: Mrs. Whatsit, Mrs. Who, and Mrs. Which. She itched to tell their story, whatever it was, and when she sat down to write, it was as if that story were fully formed in her mind, just waiting to be put on paper. It poured from her fingertips over the first few months of the new school year.

By this time, L'Engle had completed another novel, *Meet the Austins*, which was about to be published. It began with a sudden, tragic death, and early readers were concerned that the novel was too heavy for children or teens to read. But L'Engle felt strongly that difficult subjects should not be sugarcoated for young people.

She brought the same courageous approach to her new project, the book that eventually became *A Wrinkle in Time*, which incorporated many of the big ideas she'd been mulling over for years.

Later, as she accepted the Margaret A. Edwards Award for lifelong achievement from the American Library Association, L'Engle said, "It is still amazing to me that *A Wrinkle in Time* was considered too difficult for children. . . . The problem is not that it's too difficult for children, but that it's too difficult for grown-ups. Much of the worldview of Einstein's thinking wasn't being taught when the grown-ups were in school, but the children were comfortably familiar with it."

The science alone, however, was not what set L'Engle's work apart. It was the way she combined elements of science with elements of fantasy that made *A Wrinkle in Time* stand out. She believed firmly that facts were only one part of a true story. To be true in a deeper sense, the story also needed imagination. "Another

Pages from Madeleine L'Engle's manuscript, with editorial notes

One: MRS WHATSIT

It was a dark and stormy night.

In her attic bedroom Margaret Murry, sat on the foot of her bed, (wrapped in an old patchwork quilt,) and watched the trees tossing in the frenzied lashing of the wind. Behind the trees clouds scudded~~, seeming to move in terror~~ frantically across the sky~~; and every once in a while~~ EVERY FEW MOMENTS The moon the moon ~~would glimmer through a tear in the clouds, giving a feeble and frightened pretense at light~~ ripped Through them, creating wraithlike shadows That raced along The ground.

The house shook.

Wrapped ~~up~~ in her quilt Meg shook.

She wasn't usually afraid of weather. -It's not just the weather, she thought. -It's the weather on top of everything else. On top of me. On top of Meg Murry doing everything wrong.

School. School was all wrong. She'd been dropped down to the lowest section in her grade. That morning one of her teachers had said crossly, "Really, Meg, I do understand how a child with parents as brilliant as are supposed to be can be such a poor student. If y manage to do a little better you'll have to stay bac year."

During lunch she'd rough-housed a little to t make herself feel better, and one of the girls said fully, "After all, Meg, we aren't grammar school kid more. Why do you always act like such a baby?"

And on the way home from school, walking up

with her arms full of books, one of the boys had said something about her "dumb baby brother." ~~and~~ At This she'd thrown the books on the side of the road and tackled him with every ounce of strength she had, and arrived home with her blouse torn and a big bruise under one eye.

Sandy and Dennys, her ten year old twin brothers, who got home from school an hour earlier than she did, were disgusted. "Let us do the fighting when it's necessary," they told her.

-A delinquent, that's what I am, she thought grimly. -That's what they'll be saying next. Not Mother. But Them. Everybody Else. I wish Father --

But it was still not possible to think about her father without the danger of tears. Only her mother could talk about him in a natural way, saying, "When your father gets back -- "

Gets back from where? And when? Surely ~~Mrs. Murry~~ her moTher must know what people were saying, must be aware of the smugly vicious gossip. Surely it must hurt her as it did Meg. But if it did she gave no outward sign. Nothing ruffled the serenity of her expression.

-Why can't I hide it, too? Meg thought. -Why do I always have to show everything?

~~Her~~ The window rattled madly in the wind, and she pulled the quilt ~~more~~ close~~ly~~ about her. Curled up on one of her pillows a grey fluff of kitten yawned, showing its pink tongue, tucked its head under again, and went back to sleep.

Everybody was asleep. Everybody except Meg. Even

Charles Wallace, the "dumb baby brother", who had an uncanny way of knowing when she was awake and unhappy, and who would come, so many nights, tiptoing up the attic stairs to her, even Charles Wallace was asleep.

How could they sleep? All day on the radio there had been hurricane warnings. How could they leave her up in the attic in the rickety brass bed, knowing that the roof might be blown right off the house, and she tossed out into the wild night sky to land who knows where?

Her shivering grew uncontrollable.

-You asked to have the attic bedroom, she told herself savagely. -Mother let you have it because you're the oldest. It's a privelege, not a punishment.

"Not during a hurricane, it isn't a privelege," she said aloud, she tossed the quilt down on the foot of the bed, and stood up. The kitten stretched luxuriously, and looked up at her with huge, innocent eyes.

"Go back to sleep," Meg said. "Just be glad you're a kitten and not a monster like me." She looked at herself in the wardrobe mirror and made a horrible face, baring a mouthful of ~~crooked~~ teeth ~~[illegible]~~ covered with braces. Automatically She pushed her glasses ~~up her nose~~ into position, ran her fingers through her mouse-brown hair, so that it stood wildly on end, and let out a sigh almost as noisy as the wind.

The wide wooden floorboards were cold against her feet. Wind blew in the crevices about the window frame, in spite of the protection the storm sash was supposed to offer. She could hear wind howling in the chimneys.

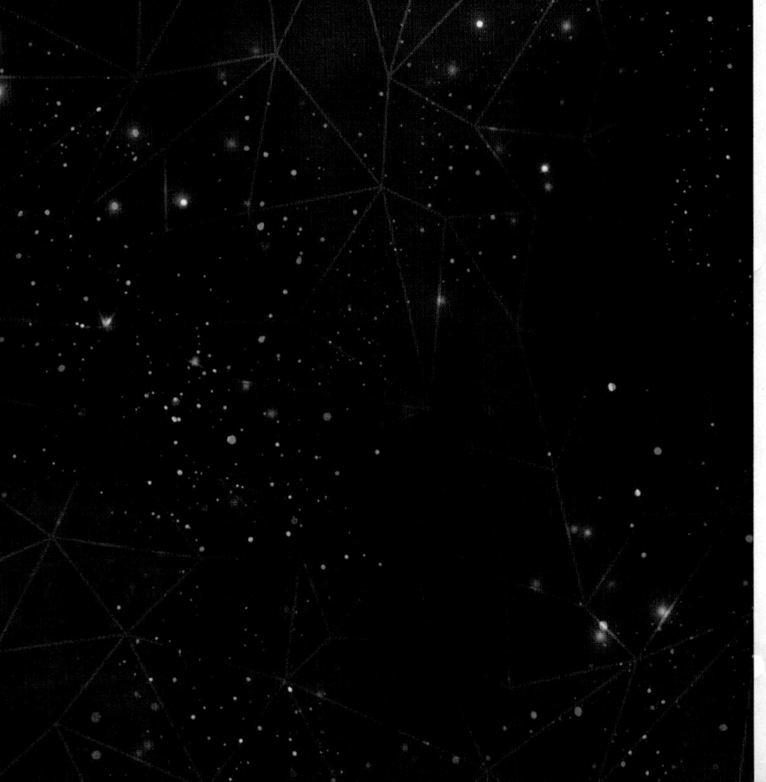

3.

Charles Wallace, the "dumb baby brother", who had an uncanny way of knowing when she was awake and unhappy, and who would come, so many nights, tiptoing up the attic stairs to her, even Charles Wallace was asleep.

How could they sleep? All day on the radio there had been hurricane warnings. How could they leave her up in the attic in the rickety brass bed, knowing that the roof might be blown right off the house, and she tossed out into the wild night sky to land who knows where?

Her shivering grew uncontrollable.

-You asked to have the attic bedroom, she told herself savagely. -Mother let you have it because you're the oldest. It's a privelege, not a punishment.

"Not during a hurricane, it isn't a privelege," she said aloud, she tossed the quilt down on the foot of the bed, and stood up. The kitten stretched luxuriously, and looked up at her with huge, innocent eyes.

"Go back to sleep," Meg said. "Just be glad you're a kitten and not a monster like me." She looked at herself in the wardrobe mirror and made a horrible face, baring a mouthful of ~~crooked~~ teeth ~~[illegible]~~ covered with braces. Automatically She pushed her glasses ~~up her nose~~ into position, ran her fingers through her mouse-brown hair, so that it stood wildly on end, and let out a sigh almost as noisy as the wind.

The wide wooden floorboards were cold against her feet. Wind blew in the crevices about the window frame, in spite of the protection the storm sash was supposed to offer. She could hear wind howling in the chimneys.

assumption was that science and fantasy don't mix," L'Engle said. "Why not? . . . Often the only way to look clearly at this extraordinary universe is through fantasy, fairy tale, myth."

L'Engle's new manuscript married real science with imagined planets. What's more, the whole story was told from the point of view of a difficult young girl. "One of the unwritten rules of science fiction was that the protagonist should be male," L'Engle said. "Why would I give all the best ideas to a male?"

> "It's a book that pushes your imagination to the next level. It doesn't follow a normal film structure in any way. It's very ethereal and spiritual, and it . . . gets in your head."
>
> **–JENNIFER LEE, SCREENWRITER**

Meg was smart, stubborn, persistent, and occasionally unpleasant. She had little in common with female characters in other books published at this time, and still less in common with the ideal girl of the early 1960s. Meg was not cheerful, she was not submissive, and she did not focus on fitting in.

"Meg is a really wonderful role model for girls because she's not perfect," Jones Voiklis said. "She is awkward, she feels out of place, she loses her temper, she gets into fights, and she feels alone and misunderstood. Reading a story about a young person dealing with these things who is able to grow and realize that her anger and stubbornness, things she believed were her faults, are actually the things that are going to help save the universe, can be very powerful."

Because of its unusual nature, perhaps, it took a long time for *A Wrinkle in Time* to find a publisher. For two years, L'Engle's literary agent shared it with editors and received rejection after rejection. Some of these rejections came with advice to revise the manuscript, but L'Engle didn't want to compromise her vision for the book. Finally, after twenty-six editors turned it down, John Farrar of Farrar, Straus and Giroux decided to take a risk on it. He expected only modest sales for the book, but he saw the quality of L'Engle's writing and the potential in her story. Maybe it was just different enough from other books that it would find an audience, he hoped.

Published in 1962, *A Wrinkle in Time* received mixed reviews from critics, but it connected right away with readers.

As of today, *A Wrinkle in Time* has sold millions of copies in thirty-two languages. In 1963, it won the Newbery Medal, the highest achievement for a children's book, and L'Engle delivered a memorable speech upon accepting her award.

"Up on the summit of Mohawk Mountain in northwest Connecticut," she remembered, "is a large flat rock that holds the heat of the sun long after the last of the late sunset has left the sky. We take our picnic up there and then lie on the rock and watch the stars, one pulsing slowly into the deepening blue, and then another and another and another until the sky is full of them. A book, too, can be a star, 'explosive material, capable of stirring up fresh life endlessly,' a living fire to lighten the darkness, leading out into the expanding universe."

With her poetic language, her creative blend of science and fantasy, and her unforgettable characters, L'Engle continued to inspire readers and writers for the rest of her life. After *A Wrinkle in Time*, she wrote a number of interconnected novels that won awards in their own right. *A Wind in the Door*, *A Swiftly Tilting Planet*, *Many Waters*, and *An Acceptable Time* track the further adventures of the Murry family, and the Murrys also appear in some of L'Engle's other work. L'Engle published many volumes of nonfiction, became a noted lecturer around the world, and served for decades as the librarian and writer-in-residence at New York's Cathedral of Saint John the Divine. Even in the heart of that grand and sacred space, L'Engle's fans sought her out.

The four other titles in the Time Quintet

Jones Voiklis has this explanation for why her grandmother's book has stood the test of time: "I think it's just as relevant today as it ever was. It's a story about a girl who travels the universe in search of her father, believing that he is going to make everything all better, only to realize that she has the tools herself. She needs to make the changes she envisions herself."

This powerful, universal message guaranteed that the book would resonate with readers for generations.

Also, inevitably, it attracted the attention of Hollywood's finest filmmakers.

Producers Jim Whitaker and Catherine Hand on-set with director Ava DuVernay and a crew member

Dr. Alex Murry with a young Meg

Ava DuVernay looks over material with co-producer Adam Borba

Meg in her attic bedroom

Early concept artwork of Calvin and Meg's perilous trek on the planet of Camazotz

CHAPTER TWO
THE WORLD OF THE FILM

The bright planet moved out of their vision. For a moment there was the darkness of space; then another planet. The outlines of this planet were not clean and clear. It seemed to be covered with a smoky haze. Through the haze Meg thought she could make out the familiar outlines of continents like pictures in her Social Studies books.

"Is it because of our atmosphere that we can't see properly?" she asked anxiously.

"Nno, Mmegg, yyou knnoww thatt itt iss nnott tthee attmossphheeere," Mrs Which said. "Yyou mmusstt bee brrave."

"It's the Thing!" Charles Wallace cried. "It's the Dark Thing we saw from the mountain peak on Uriel."

—Madeleine L'Engle, *A Wrinkle in Time*

The Newbery transformed Madeleine L'Engle's life as a writer and gained her a broad new base of readers. And it was because of the award that the book fell for the first time into the hands of film producer Catherine Hand.

Hand was in fifth grade when she was sent to the school library for talking too much in class. The librarian handed her a book to read, pointing out that it had just won the Newbery. Hand had no idea what the shiny medal pasted on the cover meant, but she loved the book from the first page. She saw herself—and her faults—in Meg. She saw her family in Meg's family. And as soon as she finished the book, she began a letter to Walt Disney himself, explaining why this book would make a perfect movie.

Hand never sent that letter, but the idea always stayed with her. When Walt Disney died on December 15, 1966, Hand wished she'd told him about her favorite book. She made a promise that day, though: Since Walt Disney couldn't make the movie, she would. Fifty years later—almost to the day—she was on location with the cast and crew.

Producer Catherine Hand

Hand first negotiated for the film rights when she was working as an assistant to Norman Lear, the iconic producer of television series such as *All in the Family*. A friend asked her what she would like to produce, if she ever had the chance, and Hand had her answer ready: *A Wrinkle in Time*. She gave the book to her friend to read, and he liked it. "It's a cross between *Star Wars* and *The Wizard of Oz*," he said. His response gave Hand the confidence to take the book to Lear himself.

Lear loved the novel, but he cautioned Hand that a visionary filmmaker would be necessary to bring it to life on screen due to its otherworldly settings and serious themes. The first hurdle, though, was obtaining the rights from L'Engle. Others had tried and failed, unwilling to agree to the author's terms. She had developed a fearsome reputation.

But Hand and L'Engle had a connection from the moment they met over lunch at Windows on the World, the restaurant and observatory on the top floor of New York's World Trade Center North Tower. Hand remembers, "The restaurant had the most awesome view of the city, and *A Wrinkle in Time* had the most awesome view of the universe—I thought it was a perfect match." Within months, Hand and L'Engle had come to an agreement and begun a lasting friendship (though later L'Engle would admit the chief reason she agreed to that first meeting was that she wanted to eat at Windows on the World!).

The road ahead was longer and windier than Hand ever could have imagined. There were many stops and starts, with multiple scripts written and countless people attached to the project over decades. The novel was difficult to adapt because it contained so many elements: science, travel, friendship, good and evil, to name a few. In addition, film companies merged and split, changing the course of production. Through it all, Hand remained steadfast in her belief that a film could—and would—"reflect the beauty and awe of the book," as she put it. A 2003 television version of the story that she produced did not quite fit the bill, Hand felt. So she kept pushing for a major motion picture to be made.

"I am in awe of Catherine's determination, persistence, stubbornness, and faith, all traits that Meg possesses as well," Jones Voiklis said. Even when Hand was working outside the film industry, she was still cultivating potential partners for the film.

A 2004 split between Miramax and The Walt Disney Company left Disney in control of the rights for the film. And when producer Jim Whitaker approached the studio with his interest in *A Wrinkle in Time*, executive Tendo Nagenda knew the perfect partner for him: Catherine Hand.

Hand was deeply moved by a documentary Whitaker had made for the 9/11 memorial in New York, and the two bonded further about what might work—or not work—in a script for *A Wrinkle in Time.*

Chris Pine takes a moment on-set with producer Jim Whitaker

They were looking for the perfect writer when the perfect writer came to them. Jennifer Lee, the writer of megahit *Frozen,* wanted to be considered because *A Wrinkle in Time* was her favorite book from childhood.

"I think I was nine the first time I read it, and it was my first introduction to science fiction, it was my first introduction to a character who was dynamic and flawed and unique," Lee said. "Meg was not the pretty one in the class, and she didn't go through a makeover to be pretty. She went through this extraordinary adventure and came out stronger as a person, and it defied anything that I'd ever read—so I was hooked."

She made a point of rereading it every year and could hardly wait to introduce her daughter to her favorite book. "I read it to her at eight, and then she reread it in school at ten, and that was right when I heard that Disney was looking for a writer."

The first time Lee met with Whitaker, the two had a far-reaching conversation that kept circling back to L'Engle's book, Lee remembers. "We talked about Meg, this extraordinary girl. We talked about physics, we talked about the universe, we talked about all this incredible stuff, and our sensibilities really fit."

"What makes *Wrinkle* really special is that it's not trying to just show a battle between light and dark, where light wins. It's saying that in life we are both, and that we can learn to balance the darkness and serve the light. It's teaching us to embrace all that we are."

—JENNIFER LEE, SCREENWRITER

Lee's next meeting was with Hand and Nagenda; they, too, bonded over their love for the novel. While she was not yet officially part of the team, Lee could imagine how she would adapt L'Engle's work for the screen.

"We first met her in April 2014, and she immediately reminded me of a young Madeleine," Hand said. Lee was juggling many commitments, but Disney gave her special permission to add *Wrinkle* to her full plate because she was so clearly the right fit.

When she sat down to write, Lee said, she gave herself some stern advice. "The most important thing I said to myself was, 'This is a film.' I'm not just trying to put the book on screen. I couldn't do that—I couldn't do it justice. The film can never be the book. But what it can be—if we work hard—is what the book makes us feel. It can be those moments in the book that are everything to us, those characters that are everything to us. We can bring them to the screen with the same feelings and know and accept that we're doing an adaptation."

Because a film audience sees characters from the outside—rather than experiencing their interior lives, as when reading a book—Lee thought hard about how to communicate Meg's emotional journey. "In the book, we get to be inside

A thoughtful Meg Murry

her head, and it's a wonderful mess in there. But a film is all about what you can see and say, so how you interpret that in a way that's evocative and just as emotional is a great challenge."

In discussing Charles Wallace Murry, Meg's precocious—and perhaps psychic—little brother, Lee said, "Charles Wallace is a kid that isn't afraid to speak his mind. He's a little arrogant for his age and gets himself in trouble because of that. There's something special about him, and what makes him special also makes him vulnerable."

While Calvin O'Keefe, the popular

Charles Wallace Murry

Meg Murry and Calvin O'Keefe

Dr. Alex Murry and Dr. Kate Murry

neighborhood boy from a difficult home, was older than Charles Wallace, Lee felt he was even more fragile in some ways. "Calvin is a kid who's desperate for love, and we all know that kid. When the IT realizes that and really takes him down, it breaks my heart."

To the screenwriter, Mrs. Murry was relatable as a parent. "Mrs. Murry is a brilliant scientist, but she's also a working mom, and she's juggling everything. She's trying to keep the spirit of her kids going as their father is missing, and that is really challenging and very painful."

Her script would need to distinguish among the Mrs.'s in style and speech. "Mrs. Whatsit is the youngest," Lee explained. "She is really connected to her life as a star—she kind of *is* a star—she's the spark. She is not so sure about Meg. She's not afraid to push on all Meg's flaws—in fact, she's pretty focused on them. We all need that person in our lives that makes us confront our own weaknesses."

Three celestial beings take Meg on an intergalactic adventure. Left to right: Mrs. Whatsit, Mrs. Who, Mrs. Which

On the other hand, Lee said, "The heart of Mrs. Who is that she's all love, the most caring, giving, unconditional warmth. She's like a surrogate mother when the children are not with their mother." And "Mrs. Which is almost as old as time. She's the oldest, the wisest, but she's also the most majestic and beautiful, and she's always thinking in terms of time. Of all we want to achieve, and all that we want to do, but how little time we have."

A lifelong fan of *A Wrinkle of Time,* Lee had been given a once-in-a-lifetime chance to show what she had previously only imagined. It was amazing to think that "we would choose what creature Mrs. Whatsit looks like when she transforms. We would decide what Uriel would look like." With each decision, Lee remembered her responsibility to evoke the same feelings as the book—even if that meant changing some of the details.

The Happy Medium looking inquisitive

She realized, for instance, that there was an opportunity to make Meg's meeting with the Happy Medium more visual than it was on the page. "In the book, the Happy Medium is a fortune-teller, and you don't get a lot of visuals from that. But the concept of a happy medium is about balance in your life, and so we've completely reinterpreted it so that the Happy Medium is in this place that is the most complicated system of balance. Wonderful sculptures, complicated balance beams, and things. It's a world the characters have to learn to balance in in order to succeed at what they're trying to do. It's the same idea as in the book, but actualized in a way that you feel when you watch it."

And throughout her script, Lee tried to preserve the humor of L'Engle's novel. "My favorite humor comes from the characters, not because they are telling jokes. We take these kids and throw them out into the universe, and they have real kid reactions—the sarcasm, the look-at-this absurdity. It was there for us to mine from the book, and the actors inspired us as well to build organic humor, right on the spur of the moment."

The Murry family has a late-night visitor. Left to right: Mrs. Murry, Charles Wallace, and Meg

By the end of 2015, Lee's screenplay was complete, and the production team was in place. The film's future looked bright. . . . And it was brighter yet when a groundbreaking director came forward to take part in the project.

Ava DuVernay began her career in journalism and public relations, but she eventually managed to achieve her lifelong dream of directing movies. An African American woman in an industry

Jim Whitaker, Ava DuVernay, and crew on-set

Calvin gets a rare smile from Meg at school

dominated by men, DuVernay was recognized for her vision and work ethic. Her first films were documentaries, but by the time Hand and Nagenda met her, she was well known as a feature director. DuVernay's second feature film, *Middle of Nowhere*, earned her the best director award at the Sundance Film Festival in 2012. And *Selma*, her movie about Dr. Martin Luther King Jr. and the 1965 march from Selma to Montgomery, received two Academy Award nominations, including best picture, in 2014.

DuVernay did not know *A Wrinkle in Time* from childhood, but she fell in love with it as an adult. "I was looking for something new when this script came to me, and as soon as I read it I felt like it was mine." She added, "When I read it, I knew what I wanted it to be. I knew how I wanted to tell it and I just took total ownership of it. I wanted to present it to the world in a fresh new way. Excitement isn't even the word—it is truly one of the thrills of my life to be working on this film." She would be the first female African American director with a budget of $100 million.

She embraced the challenge of creating new worlds and adapting a beloved novel, but above all she connected to the message buried in the heart of the story. It spoke to DuVernay's professional and personal development, and she felt sure it would connect with all kinds of audiences as well.

The director explained: "One of the things girls are taught as children is to wait for permission. Wait for permission to cross the street, wait for permission before you eat, wait for permission before it's time to go to school, or whatever it is that you want to do. But when you become an adult and you're really getting into your work life and into pursuing your passions, it becomes inhibiting to wait for permission. For me, it was really important to give myself permission to do the things I wanted to do, and I think if we encourage each other to do more work

Inside the Happy Medium's cave

from a place of passion, then we'll get a lot further and we'll have a lot more people living their dreams.

"*A Wrinkle in Time* is this beautiful stew of delicious ingredients," DuVernay said with contagious enthusiasm. "Adventure, science, romance, social commentary, spirituality—it's an epic journey that really attracted me as a filmmaker. We don't often see girls at the center of a story, certainly not girls of color, multicultural casts, all different kinds of worlds and planets. It is really something out of my wildest imagination."

L'Engle's granddaughter was also delighted with the choice of director. Jones Voiklis said, "I knew she was the right person to direct this movie after watching *Selma* and *13th*. It was such an exciting

"To see Ava manage with such grace and such assurance, all these men and women and people from everywhere, and all these machines . . . wow. It makes me proud to spell my name woman. That's what seeing her every day does for me. It makes me proud to spell my name W-O-M-A-N."

—OPRAH WINFREY,
MRS. WHICH

choice for a director . . . She represents so many firsts, as did my grandmother, and I think the two mirror each other beautifully. One of the things my grandmother would always say is that we can't pretend evil doesn't exist. We need to give children the tools with which to fight it. Ava understands that as well, and goes about it with a great clarity of vision and empathy."

With a top-notch script and director poised to make history, *A Wrinkle in Time* was ready to go into production.

Concept artwork of Camazotz

"It was amazing to think we would choose what creature Mrs. Whatsit looks like when she transforms. We would decide what Uriel would look like."

—JENNIFER LEE, SCREENWRITER

Dr. Alex Murry is held in a small, escape-proof room on Camazotz

Meg and her mother

Ava DuVernay shares a moment with Deric McCabe

Meg holds her locket on the basketball court

"We are our light and our dark,
—MRS. WHO

made whole by our love."

Meg's enfolder

Meg learning to balance with the Happy Medium

Storm Reid on set with director Ava DuVernay

CHAPTER THREE
FIRST STEPS

"Sso nnow wee ggo," Mrs Which said. "Tthere iss nott all thee ttime inn tthe worrlld."

"Could we hold hands?" Meg asked.

"You can try," Mrs Whatsit said, "though I'm not sure how it will work. You see, though we travel together, we travel alone. We will go first and take you afterward in the backwash. That may be easier for you." As she spoke the great white body began to waver, the wings to dissolve into mist. Mrs Who seemed to evaporate until there was nothing left but the glasses, and then the glasses, too, disappeared."

—Madeleine L'Engle, *A Wrinkle in Time*

Beginning film production is a complex process. The director and producers must find actors to embody the characters, of course, while also establishing what the film will look like. Ava DuVernay and her team began work on both fronts at the same time, the casting and design decisions working in tandem to influence and challenge each other.

From her first reading of the script, she envisioned a multiracial cast to bring L'Engle's timeless story into a recognizable present, and finding the right Meg was key. DuVernay and her team reviewed thousands of audition tapes, but young Storm Reid stood out from the start. Reid had made her feature film debut in Steve McQueen's Academy Award–winning *Twelve Years a Slave*, and the young girl had worked steadily since that time, growing in stature and experience as an actor. DuVernay saw how this thirteen-year-old could convey her contemporary and universal vision from the first moments of the film. "Storm Reid as Meg is a departure from the description of the girl in the book," DuVernay says. "She's a biracial child and so this is a girl who's inclusive

"Ava says that Meg is everyone. When you're with Meg, you feel safe because she is messy and flawed and she's got pain and she's struggling to find her way in the world."

—JENNIFER LEE, SCREENWRITER

Meg Murry with her beloved locket, which holds a picture of her missing father

of all different kinds of people. The hope is that you see this film, no matter who you are, and you see yourself in it. The real world is made up of all kinds of folks. It's a quilt, you know, it's a tapestry, and we all have a thread within it."

As they began to work together, DuVernay found inspiration in the young actor, as well. She says, "Storm is a singular talent. Every day my jaw drops at what this young woman is able to do as an actor. I mean, she can do it all. In this movie, she gets to do what so many actresses of any age don't get to do: have a full range of emotion. She's a romantic lead, she's a heroine, she has action, she gets to save the day, cry, laugh, have ego, be impatient, be forgiving, be loving, be spiteful. She gets to do it all. She's in every frame of this film, and she holds it like a freaking rock."

The perfect Charles Wallace, however, was more difficult to locate, with a seven-month worldwide search culminating only three weeks before shooting began. "Charles Wallace is a young child," producer Jim Whitaker points out, "and we needed an actor able to both sides of him: the wise-beyond-his-years and the utterly vulnerable." Ultimately, casting director Aisha Coley and the rest of DuVernay's team decided on eight-year-old Deric McCabe, who was just starting out as an actor. His extraordinary range made him perfect for the part: where at first Charles Wallace seems to protect Meg, ultimately he becomes the character most in need of protection.

Zach Galifianakis, who plays the Happy Medium, says, "Ava did a really good job of casting all the kids in this movie, because there's a realness to them. I think sometimes we put the sheen on children in the movies, but Storm is playing it as real, and she broke my heart the other day when we were doing a scene, and I got kind of emotional."

Comedian Galifianakis represents one of the ways that DuVernay reimagined the original novel. "We had always wanted to cast a man as the Happy Medium because there were already so many women in the movie . . . we needed to find some great roles for the men," says Catherine Hand.

He was also one of many well-known actors that DuVernay was able to attract to *A Wrinkle in Time*. Along with Chris Pine as Dr. Alex Murry and Gugu Mbatha-Raw as Dr. Kate Murry, Galifianakis brings major star power to the film. And the extraordinary women DuVernay tapped to play the three Mrs.'s represent the many kinds of diversity the director showcases in her film.

DuVernay wanted to reflect a broad understanding of femininity in casting Mrs. Whatsit, Mrs. Who, and Mrs. Which; she wanted to cast women of different ages, body types, and races, and reflect culture and history in the clothes they wore.

The Happy Medium

"In this sphere of mythic storytelling, it's all about the hero. And what does the hero have to go through? The hero has to learn to be selfless, and give of him or herself to something bigger, outside themselves. The beautiful part about this story is it's a young girl that goes on this journey."

—CHRIS PINE, DR. ALEX MURRY

Dr. Alex Murry at work in his lab

Mindy Kaling was brought on as Mrs. Who. The multitalented Kaling got her start in the hit TV series *The Office* and went on to create and write the acclaimed sitcom *The Mindy Project*.

Joining Kaling as Mrs. Who was the Academy Award–winning actor and producer Reese Witherspoon, playing the brisker Mrs. Whatsit. "Mrs. Whatsit is very curious because she's very new to the world," Witherspoon explains. "She's the youngest of the Mrs.'s and she doesn't know how things work. She is not used to being in human form, so she's always sort of playing with things, trying to figure things out."

And the one and only world-renowned Oprah Winfrey rounded out the trio. Catherine Hand recalls, "I'll never forget the day we got a phone call from Ava asking us, 'What do you think about Oprah as Mrs. Which? What do you think about one of the wisest people in the world playing one of the wisest people in the universe? And there wasn't a moment's hesitation. We asked Ava if it was something Oprah would even consider and she said yes, which was really exciting for all of us because Oprah is the perfect Mrs. Which."

Winfrey connected with the character right away. "Mrs. Which is a supernova," she says. "An angelic cosmic being who has known Earth, part human because she's experienced it in all of her billions of years, has complete empathy and connection to all humans, but is also one with the universe and understands that love and light is all that matters. She's here to spread that message on Earth and throughout all the other planets that love is the way, and that the only way to fight darkness is to be a warrior of the light. And I get to embody the message of the warrior of the light through this character."

Winfrey adds, "I tell Meg, 'You have to be a light warrior. You have to have faith inside yourself. You have to join the right frequency. And believe, believe, believe.' When I say these words to Meg, I believe those words. I believe those words as Oprah. I believe those words as Mrs. Which. I believe those words for the planet. I believe those words for this time in history."

As DuVernay assembled this extraordinary cast, she was also engaged in conversations about the look and the feel of the film. Producer Jim Whitaker describes her process like this: "Ava wanted to include every department head to find the best way to portray every single scene as inventively as possible. At every turn, she asked, 'Have we seen this before? How can we honor the ideas in the book but also show the audience something that is different?'"

Each scene needed to be visually striking and emotionally resonant. Whitaker adds, "Ava felt it was important to begin the movie as the book began. Then, as we progressed throughout the film, it was important to her that we keep the movie as grounded as possible, to keep the urgency moving forward and keep the emotion developing."

Production designer Naomi Shohan played the key role in developing the visual

On set in the woods of Northern California—just one location that brought the Camazotz landscape to life

options for the film. She remembered reading *A Wrinkle in Time* as a girl, and what had stuck with her the most was the simple elegance of L'Engle's writing about science. "When she used an ant on a string to describe tessering—I got that. My girlfriends got that. We could all explain it to each other," she remembers. "It made us think we could understand the universe, that it was accessible and intuitive."

A production designer is the head of a film's art department, so Shohan was charged with translating feelings and ideas into elements an audience would see. "I did want people to be thrilled by the wonder of nature," she says. Each planet would have a specific nature Shohan was eager to explore. And "Ava and I connected on the idea that we live in a world with differences, and problems, with issues of race and class." The film would explore these differences visually, as well.

Shohan knew that much of the principal photography would be taking place in practical (already existing) locations rather than on sets constructed by the crew, due to DuVernay's preference and the fact that real locations tend to look more convincing on film. A team of location scouts was already looking for the perfect places to shoot. Beyond these places, though, Shohan's team needed to imagine every detail in and around them. What colors, what textures, what sizes and shapes would bring the action and the emotion to life?

Ava DuVernay reviews shots on the set during production

"I did want people to be thrilled by the wonder of nature."

—NAOMI SHOHAN, PRODUCTION DESIGNER

Creating the perfect lighting in Camazotz

Shohan and the art department looked at thousands of photos and created hundreds of boards—collages of pictures—to inspire the team and generate new ideas. The goal was to define the essence of every place and planet in the film. Then, from there, they would design the details to bring these places to life.

Meg stands her ground on the school basketball court

Calvin O'Keefe comes to Meg's defense in the school hallway

Deric McCabe prepares for a take on the streets of Los Angeles

Meg and Calvin in the Murrys' backyard

Mrs. Who

Mrs. Which

Mrs. Whatsit

A Wrinkle in Time movie poster

Dr. Alex Murry in his home lab

Dr. Kate Murry gives a speech

The crew found the perfect Murry family home while scouting neighborhoods in Los Angeles

CHAPTER FOUR
THE MURRYS' WORLD

—I'll make myself some cocoa, Meg decided.—That'll cheer me up, and if the roof blows off at least I won't go off with it.

In the kitchen a light was already on, and Charles Wallace was sitting at the table drinking milk and eating bread and jam. He looked very small and vulnerable sitting there alone in the big old-fashioned kitchen, a blond little boy in faded blue Dr. Dentons, his feet swinging a good six inches above the floor.

"Hi," he said cheerfully. "I've been waiting for you."

—Madeleine L'Engle,
A Wrinkle in Time

Production designer Naomi Shohan describes Meg Murry's home quite simply. "The whole place is like an embrace," she says. "The warmest, most welcoming place you can imagine." The house reflects the family's varied interests, their abundant curiosity. In every room, there's evidence of some project in progress, some idea pursued.

In real life, Shohan and her team knew what homes like this would look like—they could picture what the Murrys' furniture or belongings might be. First, though, they had to find an existing house that fit their needs and would welcome a film crew for an extended stay.

Supervising location manager Alison Taylor spearheaded the effort to find the right house. "The Murrys are scientists, but they aren't necessarily wealthy," she explains. "They live in a multiracial neighborhood with other professional people like them." Since the production was based in Los Angeles, the crew canvassed areas in nearby Pasadena and Altadena, where there might be neighborhoods with this character. Eventually, director DuVernay herself suggested West Adams, a Los Angeles district of century-old Craftsman houses with a diverse and prosperous population. There,

Meg called into the school principal's office

Taylor's crew found the perfect house, and its residents loved *A Wrinkle in Time* and were willing to work with the filmmakers.

"The rooms were large, with welcoming dimensions," says Shohan, the production designer. "And the layout was right," adds Alison Taylor. "You could see the lab from the kitchen, and Mrs. Whatsit from the stairway." The art department would make adjustments to the house, but this basic geography would work for the cameras. In addition, since this house was near a school and other houses, it would be plausible that Meg, Calvin, and Charles Wallace could walk from one place to another on their own.

The residents of the house moved out for three months, all for a two-week shoot. It took three weeks to prepare it to look like the Murrys lived there, and no detail was too small to escape the notice of Shohan's team.

Set decorator Elizabeth Keenan remembers, "Ava, Naomi, and I talked at length about the Murry characters and how we should visually tell their story, making this film look unique while being respectful to the classic, well-loved book. The Murry house itself is almost another character. Education and travel are more important to this family than acquiring material goods, thus the home reflects a broad mixture of cultural and scientific interests, with music being a central focus."

Within the house, she decorated several individual rooms, from the kitchen to the family's bedrooms. "For the set of Meg's attic bedroom, it was important to depict that occupying that specific room was a privilege and not teenage exile," says Keenan. "We carved out a niche for her amongst family storage and items left over from childhood,

> "We covered her attic bedroom walls with book reports, school projects, and posters of strong, intellectual female images."
>
> —ELIZABETH KEENAN, SET DECORATOR

including the old ping-pong table and rocking horse noted in Madeleine L'Engle's book. We covered her attic bedroom walls with book reports, school projects, and posters of strong, intellectual female images in the areas of mathematics and the sciences: a poster from an Ada Byron Lovelace play, images of astronaut Dr. Mae C. Jemison, mathematician Marjorie Lee Browne, physicist Katherine Johnson, Shirley Ann Jackson, and more. A

Meg's attic bedroom is cozy and bright, with books, science projects, and photos of inspirational women displayed all around

Charles Wallace's bedroom was meant to convey his intelligence and old soul, without betraying his young age

> "The set of Charles Wallace's room needed to communicate a spirit wise beyond his physical years."
>
> —**ELIZABETH KEENAN, SET DECORATOR**

love of Einstein, Carl Sagan, and Kurt Vonnegut would have also inspired her and helped guide her self-discovery."

On the other hand, "The set of Charles Wallace's room needed to communicate a spirit wise beyond his physical years. He has an immense amount of insight and knowledge for his age," says Keenan. "Is he otherworldly? We don't really know. Instead of toys Charles has loads of books, loads of Hubble images, a mineral collection, and lots of interesting projects he's working on littered around the room, and his workbench and desk overlooks the home lab so he can keep an eye on his mother."

Knickknacks and toys in Charles Wallace's bedroom

Charles Wallace's desk, covered with scientific items

The Murry family home lab

The crew used the house's garage—which had been used for storage—to build the Murrys' lab. Elizabeth Keenan continues, "The Murry home and home lab obviously needed to accurately portray the parents' different professions, and for this specific project I hired a recent Mount Holyoke astronomy and geology graduate, Claire Schwartz, as a Set Dec PA to help navigate this unfamiliar terrain. As she had previously worked at several JPL and CalTech labs, Claire was instrumental in allowing us access to astrophysicists, geologists, and other scientists at both institutions. We eventually hired Dr. Rohit Bhartia, Ph.D., from JPL as our technical adviser for the Murry home lab and the father's tessering scenes."

Keenan continues, "For the home

> "Working on this story is very complicated. Logistically you're trying to defy people's imaginations, but you're also trying to ground it in something real . . . Everything has to serve this emotional adventure that we're going on."
>
> —JENNIFER LEE, SCREENWRITER

lab set, the ideas to use the HAG Capisco stools, huge 1,000-pound Newport smart tables (on casters for ease of movement), Formlabs 3-D printer, and the Ophir-Spiricon equipment all originated from these field visits. Disney's Lauren Thomas was indispensible in obtaining product placement for a lot of these astronomically expensive and specialized lab pieces."

And she never lost sight of where in the country this house existed. "Attached to the overhead lab shelving you'll notice straps holding in the jammed periodicals and textbooks. That was a California earthquake detail prevalent in several of the labs we visited," she says.

Meg Murry and Calvin O'Keefe in the thick of their adventure

One goal of the set decoration was to create links between parts of the film. To that end, Keenan explains, "There are little visual themes throughout the house . . . the planetary shape of the drapery finials, the four-globe fixture in the upstairs hallway (Earth, Uriel, Ixchel, and Camazotz), and the cluster of lanterns over the dining room table relates back to a classroom scene with student-made molecular structures. There is a conceptual reason for every decorating decision in this film. Whether the audience notices or not, it creates an unconscious visual storytelling."

The Murrys' costumes were chosen to tie in with the general feeling of the home, as well. Dr. Kate Murry, the children's mother, "is a good mother, but enclosed into herself," says costume designer Paco Delgado. "She is having a hard time." Viewers will see Dr. Murry wrapped in knitted cardigans—"beautiful, but not glamorous," says Delgado. "Her unsophisticated, normal outfit creates contrast between this reality and the fantasy world we see later."

At the same time, Delgado explains, "There is very simple costuming for the kids. They wear what kids wear: jeans and T-shirts and flannels. And the costumes don't really change throughout the film because, you know, they aren't traveling with a suitcase."

The Murrys' costumes—and the characters wearing them—remain consistent even when the story calls for them to enter extraordinary new worlds.

The anniversary of her father's disappearance is never an easy day for Meg

Murry family dog, Fortinbras

Calvin reads to Charles Wallace

Meg's locket

The Murry family in happier times, years before Mr. Murry's disappearance

Early exploration of Meg's enfolder

As the enfolder is used, the size of the heart grows

Mrs. Who's "haunted house" is as eccentric, eclectic, and worldly as the celestial woman herself

CHAPTER FIVE
THE MRS.'S WORLD

"I'm not talking about my mother's feelings about my father," Charles Wallace scolded. "I'm talking about Mrs. Buncombe's sheets."

The little woman sighed. The enormous glasses caught the light again and shone like an owl's eyes. "In case we need ghosts, of course," she said. "I should think you'd have guessed. If we have to frighten anybody away Whatsit thought we ought to do it appropriately. That's why it's so much fun to stay in a haunted house. But we really didn't mean you to know about the sheets."

—Madeleine L'Engle, *A Wrinkle in Time*

The Earthly home occupied by Mrs. Who isn't actually her home. Still, Ava DuVernay's team made sure to imagine it thoroughly, as this house is a way station between Earth—where things are predictable and familiar—and a series of other planets, where they are not. "We found the house in a neighborhood adjacent to West Adams," production designer Naomi Shohan says. "The houses there have similar architecture, but they're smaller. And the one we shot was a derelict house, almost like a haunted house. It was a perfect echo of what we found in the text."

Because Mrs. Who speaks almost exclusively in quotes, Keenan's team filled this house with books, as if Mrs. Who draws words from her personal library. Clues abound, however, that this is no ordinary library or ordinary house. Books are set in piles that are gravitationally impossible, and a tree grows out of the middle of a piano. "You can think of it as the tree of knowledge," says Shohan. "As if some of the film's themes are planted in this room."

Stacks of books wind their way through Mrs. Who's home

Costume designer Paco Delgado embraced the challenge of dressing the Mrs.'s. "Every character has a style of their own," he explains, "but every planet influences what they are wearing. Like the way you'd have one wardrobe for winter in Oslo, one wardrobe for vacation in Hawaii." On Earth, then, the Mrs.'s are dressed in Earth fabrics and styles, but their outfits become more out of this world as the film goes on.

Because Mrs. Whatsit is supposed to be stealing sheets, says Delgado, "we came up with this abstract idea of white material being folded around her, so it looks a little like sheets and a little like a garment. The material is very folded. We practiced folding material around a dummy to see what kind of plasticity we could get from different fabrics. Of the three, her costumes are the most abstract but also the most organic. She comes from Uriel, so she has the greatest connection with nature."

> "Meg is guided by these celestial beings, these stars, these amazing women, the Mrs.'s, who come to assist her. But, you know, we all have Mrs.'s in our lives. The Mrs.'s represent our instincts, our imagination, our education, and our experience, all of these intangibles . . . That's what the women represent, and if you hone in on the best of yourself and listen to that, then you give yourself permission to be on the journey you should be on."
>
> —AVA DuVERNAY, DIRECTOR

To reflect Mrs. Who's identity as a guardian of knowledge, Delgado drew inspiration from folktales and clothing from ethnic groups across the globe. "Ancient cultures," he says, "Japanese, Chinese, Peruvian . . . At the beginning, she's wearing a huge multicolored garment with embroidered material. It features many hand-sewn elements, some techniques drawn from haute couture, even a cape made with printed feathers."

Because Mrs. Which was born in a star explosion and became a supernova, Delgado decided that her look would be more technical than the others—harder and more futuristic. "She's pure energy," he explains, "a warrior against evil." To suggest these qualities visually, in her first scene he dressed Mrs. Which in pleated silver material looking almost like corrugated metal. "It suggests armor," says Delgado. "And light, energy, stars, the universe."

When Mrs. Which finally appears to the children, it is in the Murrys' backyard, which was filmed on an empty lot in Santa Clarita, a city just north of Los Angeles. A set was built to look identical to the back of the Murry house in West Adams—the owners of the West Adams house were astonished when they saw it—and special effects supervisor Mark Hawker set about creating real-life action that would later be enhanced with visual effects. "There were platforms buried in the ground we called ripple-makers to move them up and down," Hawker explains. Through many takes, actors Storm Reid, Deric McCabe, and Levi Miller stood on these platforms and tried to keep their balance as they rode the waves. Visual effects would make it look as if the earth itself was moving, preparing to launch them through time and into space.

Mrs. Who with Meg

"I wanted to shake hands with the universe."

—DR. ALEX MURRY

Meg, Charles Wallace, and Mrs. Whatsit

Mrs. Who and her quizzing glasses

Mrs. Whatsit

Mrs. Who's quizzing glasses

Tendo Nagenda with Jim Whitaker preparing to film at the Murry house

Mrs. Whatsit marvels at the objects in the Murry home as Charles Wallace looks on

Concept artwork of the planet Uriel

CHAPTER SIX
THE WORLD OF URIEL

[Meg] looked around rather wildly. They were standing in a sunlit field, and the air about them was moving with the delicious fragrance that comes only on the rarest of spring days when the sun's touch is gentle and the apple blossoms are just beginning to unfold.
She pushed her glasses up on her nose to reassure herself that what she was seeing was real.

—Madeleine L'Engle, *A Wrinkle in Time*

Production designer Naomi Shohan remembers her very first thoughts about the planet Uriel. "I just tried to imagine the most beautiful place I had ever been," she says. "For me, it was a valley in Montana, with snowcapped mountains and the most vivid colors. I have never forgotten what I saw there." For the characters in *A Wrinkle in Time*, Uriel is a sort of heavenly place, where they realize what is at stake in the epic battle between good and evil.

Even the most brilliant art department couldn't create a landscape like Uriel, so Alison Taylor's location team set out to find a magnificent place to film. First they scouted locations in California, near where the other filming had taken place, but there were two problems. Given the time of year they were shooting, California would not be at its most lush or green. In addition, the state had been suffering from a catastrophic drought that left the landscape depleted. Eventually, the team's attention turned toward New Zealand, which offered staggering beauty as well as generous incentives to moviemakers. "We needed to find a place that would really look like a different planet, and New Zealand fit the bill," says Taylor. "Its look is truly otherworldly."

The beautiful scenery of New Zealand

> "I just tried to imagine the most beautiful place I had ever been. For me, it was a valley in Montana, with snowcapped mountains and the most vivid colors. I have never forgotten what I saw there."
>
> —NAOMI SHOHAN, PRODUCTION DESIGNER

When the children and the Mrs.'s arrive on Uriel, Shohan's team decided, they would land in a poppy field. This was an indirect nod to *The Wizard of Oz*, with one notable difference. "Illustrator Ben Wooten came up with a beautiful painting of the place our heroes land on Uriel and a second painting of giant poppy pods growing high into the atmosphere above the planet's surface. We were all standing around admiring Ben's pictures when somebody said, 'What if the characters see the poppies waving all around them and don't realize until they fly off with Mrs. Whatsit that what looked like the world to them was actually the center of one of the pods?'" That idea provided a unique perspective and a sense of magic in the planet's environment.

Costume designer Delgado created clothing to match the landscape. "Uriel is paradise, right?" he says. "So there is more color here, more joy." Mrs. Who's costume on Uriel was inspired by her library on Earth: "It's a big paneled skirt made of paper," says Delgado, "because she has all the books in her head."

Mrs. Whatsit's costume needed special attention because it would transform with the character into a new creature. When the time for her transformation arrives, Mrs. Whatsit spins, and the layers of her clothing peel away until she becomes a sort of magic carpet that the children can ride. Special-effects manager

"Uriel is paradise, right? So there is more color here, more joy."

—PACO DELGADO,
COSTUME DESIGNER

The crew setting up equipment

Mark Hawker set up high-intensity fans to create the appearance that the clothes were blowing away. Meanwhile, he used a fishing pole to remove layers of Mrs. Whatsit's clothing as she spun. The pole would be removed in post-production, but the effect would remain.

Producer Jim Whitaker remembers the brief stay in New Zealand. "Moviemaking can be long," he says. "Shooting can go on for weeks, and things can move very slowly. But sometimes there is a magical moment like the one we had when we arrived in New Zealand. It was pure euphoria. The weather cleared and the planet that needed to be the most amazing planet presented itself just like that."

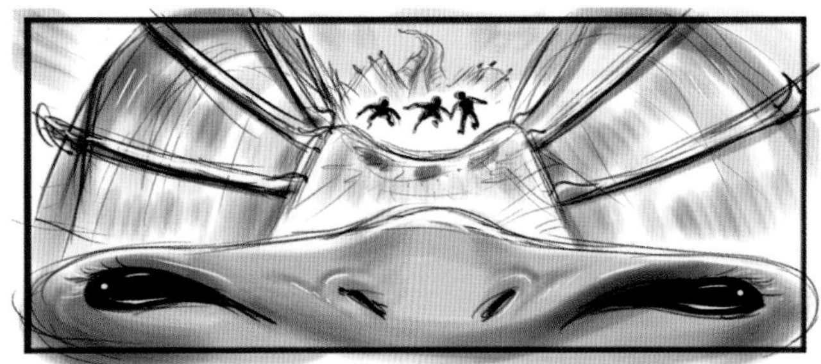

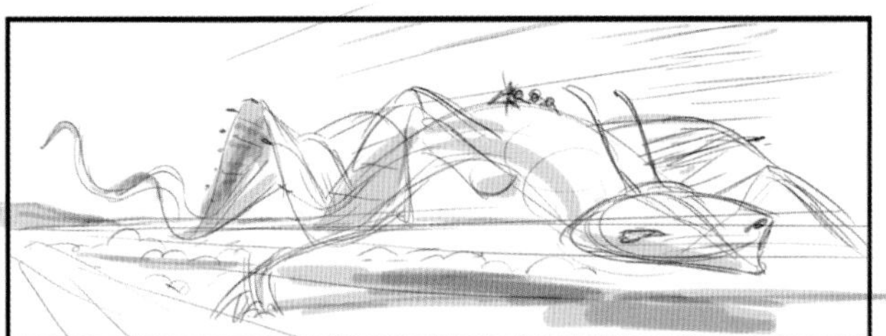

Early storyboard sketches of Creature Whatsit's flight

"You must not be afraid
—MRS. WHO

to be afraid."

Concept artwork of the planet Uriel

Early concept artwork of the planet Orion

CHAPTER SEVEN
THE WORLD OF ORION

"The shadows were swirling in the crystal again, and as they cleared Meg began to recognize her mother's lab at home. Mrs. Murry was sitting perched on her high stool, writing away at a sheet of paper on a clipboard on her lap. She's writing father, Meg thought. The way she always does. Every night."

—Madeleine L'Engle,
A Wrinkle in Time

In Madeleine L'Engle's novel, the "Happy Medium" is a play on words. Although the character is female in the book, for the film, it was decided that the Happy Medium should be male. He's a character that lives on an unnamed neutral planet that is neither large nor small, hot nor cold, black nor white. He is also a seer, a fortune-teller, a medium in the other sense of the word. The character provides critical information to Meg and Charles Wallace when he shows them a dark cloud over the planet Camazotz and confirms that their father is there. He is also everything Meg does not want to be: afraid to face the truth about the evil spreading through the universe.

Director Ava DuVernay charged her team with making the neutral planet more visually interesting. In addition, screenwriter Jennifer Lee named the planet Orion and reworked the concept of a "happy medium" in her script. Instead of just a cautionary tale, the Happy Medium provides a

The Happy Medium

model for Meg, an emotional way forward. Before they meet, Meg's emotions are wildly out of control. To achieve her goal and find her father, though, Meg needs to find some emotional balance, like the sort of physical balance she practices in the Medium's cave.

Naomi Shohan and her artists spent a good deal of time imagining what this cave might look like, and eventually it turned out to be the largest set they built for the filming of *A Wrinkle in Time*.

The first step was to imagine what the entire planet of Orion might look like.

Early concept artwork of the rocky, foggy exterior of the planet Orion

Another early concept piece of Orion from a different angle, the Happy Medium's cave in the distance

The idea of gray and neutral, from the original text, would not capture the interest of a movie audience. Shohan's team developed an alternate idea, however: that the planet is difficult to see. The atmosphere is foggy, shrouding the planet's features, and the features are gray, blending into the fog. They preserved the contrast of extremes by juxtaposing the soft fog with a rocky landscape. In the middle, then, is the cave of the Happy Medium, rich with color and open to the air.

Shohan remembers her initial inspiration for the cave itself. "We used the sandstone caves at Antelope Valley as our inspiration—they have very fluid, deeply striated contours that mold incoming light and give a dynamic sense of flow. We loved that for Orion, where we wanted an organic free-form space with a feeling of spin."

Regarding the inside of the cave, Shohan says, "The 'teeters' came from another cave, in Arizona, I think. We found a photo of tiny little people in orange hazmat

> "Ava has a welcoming way, which is helpful for someone like me—I still get intimidated by this stuff even though I've been doing it for a while."
>
> —ZACH GALIFIANAKIS, THE HAPPY MEDIUM

suits walking along these absolutely enormous crystals, like ants balancing on pencils." Eventually the idea of huge crystals in the cave evolved into an idea that the huge crystals would be moving. Shohan says, "Ava was always looking to make things more interesting, and we came up with the idea that the way to get around inside the cave would be to balance and slide on pathways of these 'teetering' crystals. Getting from one point to another was quite literally a balancing act."

Bringing this concept to life was a challenge, but the artists were able to visualize it and the crew was able to create it. "We wanted to create an upward spiral of the cave counter to the downward spirals of the teeter paths, taking care that the teeters didn't collide. After drawing

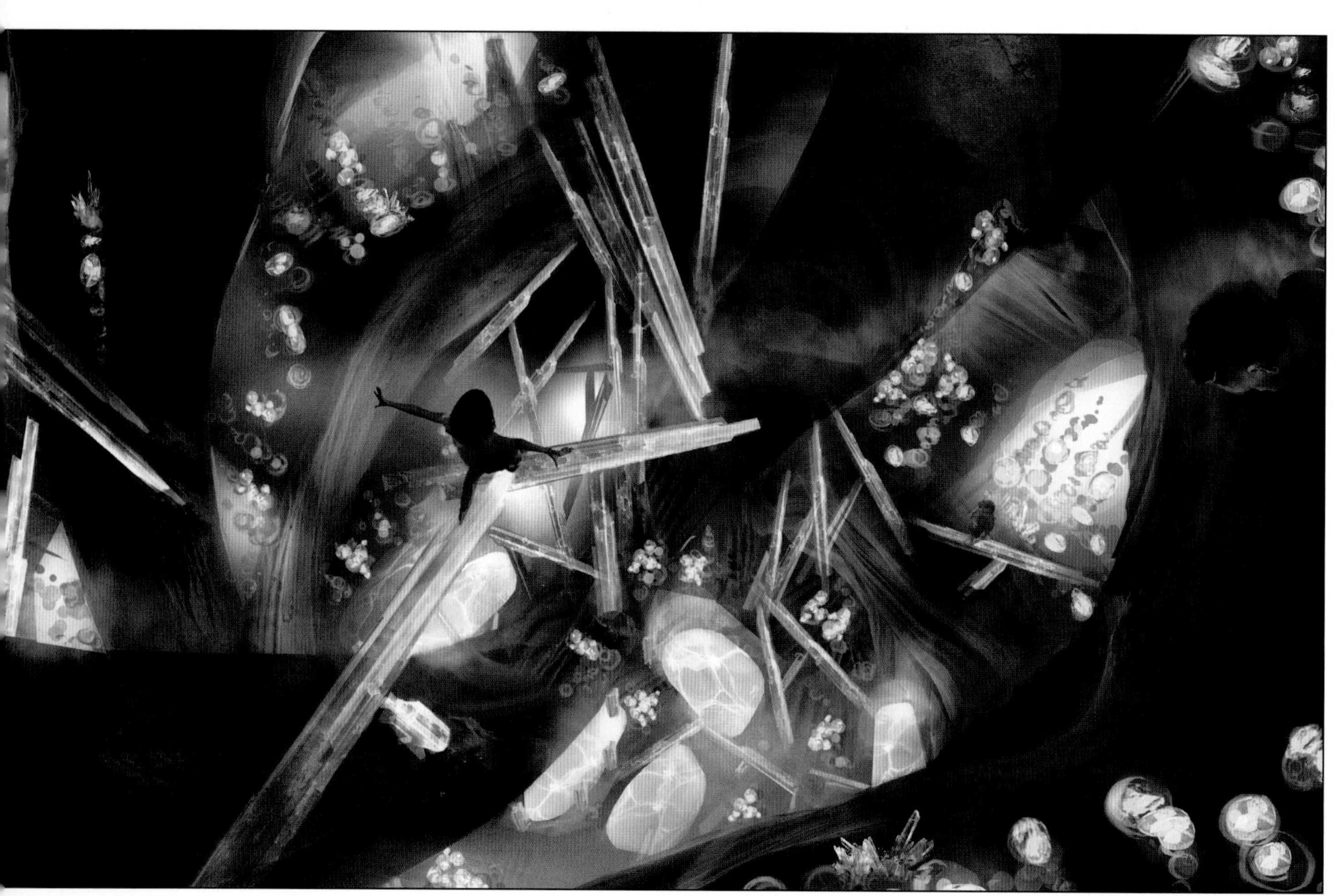

Early concept artwork of the Happy Medium's cave

the set in 3-D, we translated to a scale foam model, sliced that up, outlined the slices, replicated their contours full-scale in wood, plastered, and painted."

In L'Engle's novel, the Happy Medium is a collector of intergalactic oddities, but the art department felt that this would be difficult to translate into film. What would these oddities look like? How would an audience know what they were? "Eventually we came to the idea that the objects inside the Happy Medium's cave would be more intriguing if they were indistinct and encased in glowing amber," says Shohan. "That way we could suggest them without tripping ourselves up trying to define intergalactic curios." These pieces of amber could also be incorporated into the interior structure of the cave.

"In addition to that, we have the balancing equipment, which is made to look like amber, and there was a long period when we were carving those amber pieces, then molding and casting them—I'd say it took three to four months to build the whole thing. The characters walk along one and come down to another: they make

A rough 3-D design of the group inside the Happy Medium's cave

their descent through the cave on these giant amber seesaws. They're made out of fiberglass and they're painted from the inside with dyes. Many, many skilled people worked on the set," says the production designer.

Zach Galifianakis, who plays the Happy Medium, remembers shooting his scenes in the cave. "They really built a beautiful set," he says. "I thought it was going to be all green screen, but then Ava says, 'I want you to see the set.' So I trained with the wires and I was feeling pretty cocky, I was thinking this is easy, I can flip on these things. Then I found out I'd be flipping there . . . like, forty, forty-five feet up? I hate heights. I mean, I can't even stand on an apple box without getting vertigo."

To work with the amber interiors, Paco Delgado designed complementary amber costumes for the three Mrs.'s. His idea for the Happy Medium was inspired more by the concept of balance than by the cave's color, however: the Happy Medium wears an androgynous ensemble to suggest a balance between male and female.

The Happy Medium

Ava DuVernay points Storm Reid through a scene in the Happy Medium's cave

"The script was really well done and then Ava showed me some of the footage after the first day of work and I think the photography is breathtaking."

—ZACH GALIFIANAKIS, THE HAPPY MEDIUM

The cast worked together, though, to master the challenges of the cave and its "teeters," as they called them. When their work was done, they were ready to confront the larger tests of the planet Camazotz.

Navigating the Happy Medium's cave

"But of course we can't take any credit for our talents. It's how we use them that counts."
—MRS. WHATSIT

Early concept artwork of Meg and Calvin traversing the treacherous Camazotz terrain

CHAPTER EIGHT
THE WORLD OF CAMAZOTZ

But Mrs Whatsit came to her and put an arm around her comfortingly. "I can't stay with you here, you know, love," she said. "You three children will be on your own. We will be near you; we will be watching you. But you will not be able to see us or to ask us for help, and we will not be able to come to you." Charles Wallace looked steadily at Mrs Whatsit. "Are you afraid for us?"

"A little."

—Madeleine L'Engle, *A Wrinkle in Time*

"Camazotz was the most challenging of the planets to conceptualize," admits production designer Naomi Shohan. "I mean, how do you describe pure evil?" Her team looked at thousands of photos, searching for a spark of inspiration on how to portray the movie's villain, the literal brain center and controller of the planet: the IT. They wanted to avoid classical representations of evil. But what was left? The team wrestled with this question.

While the artists mulled over how to portray the IT, an ever-present threat that seeks to cover the universe in darkness, they began to sketch out designs for the rest of the planet, because audiences would see a few different locations on Camazotz before the final confrontation.

The first place the Murrys and their friend Calvin come to when they arrive is a seemingly innocuous

An eerie corridor on Camazotz

> "Another thing that's special about *Wrinkle* is that the power of love comes through the embracing of our flaws, the things that make us messy and make us who we are. No one should need to be perfect."
>
> **—JENNIFER LEE, SCREENWRITER**

neighborhood. It's only when they look closely that they realize something strange about it: Every house is exactly the same. Every person in every house is doing exactly the same thing at exactly the same time. The filmmakers would need to find a place to shoot such a scene, or else create it themselves.

Supervising location manager Alison Taylor had scouts looking all over California for a neighborhood of uniform houses that could be a generic suburb on any planet. There were neighborhoods with matching Spanish-tile roofs, but they were so distinctly Californian that they were unusable. It was only when scanning Google Earth that scout Pedro Mata found something promising: a tract of military housing in San Pedro. Online, he could see that the houses' roofs were identical; once his team went in and took pictures, they knew they had found the right place.

While Taylor arranged for permissions and security clearances to shoot there, the art department and set decorators went into overdrive to make every detail exactly right. The houses all had identical architecture, but there were adjustments to be made. The film crew planted grass, evened out trim, adjusted blinds, and painted sconces to make it look as if the houses were clones of one another.

Then, when it came time to shoot, the casting department had to locate multiple women and children of the exact same size and stature to populate the neighborhood. They were ethnically diverse, in keeping with DuVernay's vision, but they all had the same hairstyle, same makeup, and same costume. "It was a great example of all the departments working together," Alison Taylor recalls. "Everyone went above and beyond to make it work."

When Meg, Charles Wallace, and Calvin leave the uncanny neighborhood of identical houses, they come to a sunny beach, crowded with people. There, they meet Red, an agent of the IT whose colorful suit and welcoming smile belie a dark motive. He pretends to be a friend, even offering a delicious meal, but as they dive in they discover that the food is an illusion meant to trick them—it is all made of sand. As played by actor Michael Pena, Red is alluring and deceptive.

> "We built a giant tree trunk, maybe forty feet tall and twenty-four inches in diameter. We filled it with real branches, and we broke it in half hydraulically."
>
> **—MARK HAWKER, SPECIAL EFFECTS SUPERVISOR**

Red, an agent of the IT

Levi Miller and Storm Reid run through an action scene—literally

The IT watches everything the children do, and understands why they have come to Camazotz. As they get closer and closer to him, the IT puts more deadly—and psychologically menacing—obstacles in their way. Soon Red's appearance shifts, and the children realize he is a terrible puppet, controlled by the IT.

One of the movie's biggest action sequences also takes place on Camazotz, when the land itself conspires against the Murry children and Calvin as they attempt to get to the IT. This sequence was shot in a spectacular sequoia forest in northern California's Humboldt County. Scout Lori Balton was charged with finding trees of a certain height and density, all within a parcel of land that would allow a film crew, and she managed to find two separate parks that fit these narrow specs.

With the help of Mark Hawker, special effects supervisor, the forest appears to come to life. Meg and Calvin race through the trees until they come to a ravine. There is no way across, until a tree comes down miraculously and makes a bridge. Then the tree splits in two, as if it is trying to stop them.

"We built a giant tree trunk," says Hawker, "that was about forty feet tall and twenty-four inches in diameter. We filled it with real branches, and we broke it in half hydraulically." The cast was not in danger, but their real reactions were filmed in order to create authenticity.

Once they got past the dangers of the forest, Meg and Calvin were ready

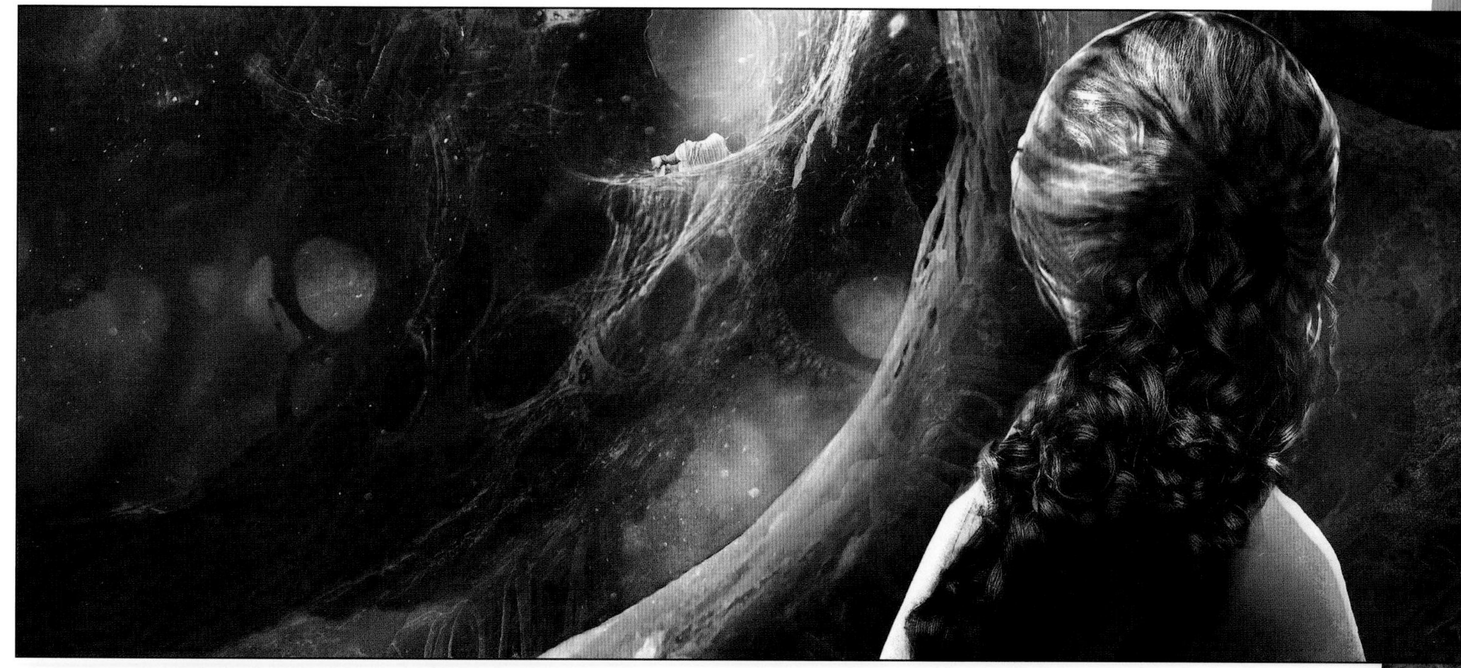

Concept artwork of the IT's dark and frightening lair

to confront the IT. "The IT is the heart and soul of Camazotz, and how to portray that was very confusing," says production designer Shohan. "We talked and talked about it, trying to figure out how to make it universal. Then somebody showed me a picture of a place called the Seed Cathedral, a U.K. entry in the 2010 Shanghai Expo. The Cathedral is composed of very long Lucite rods extending through the shell of the building from outside to form its interior walls. At the interior end of each rod is contained a small quantity of seeds, back-lit by the light traveling along its rod. The Cathedral's interior has a kind of undulating, indistinct quality. That gave us the idea of producing a space that would be equally indistinct, a space where you could never find your coordinates, that would be as close as possible to being nowhere without being entirely blank. Our set is quite different from the Seed Cathedral, but we borrowed its sense of fluctuating boundaries."

"Ultimately, what's most terrifying is not the place, but that Charles Wallace is not Charles Wallace—his mind has been consumed by the IT."

—NAOMI SHOHAN, PRODUCTION DESIGNER

Shohan and her team were able to visualize a concept of evil where the individual is completely disoriented, unmoored. Lighting designers intentionally confused the perspective so Meg would have no idea where she was or where to go within this maze.

Eventually Meg would enter the brain

The crew setting the scene

of the IT, but that was a much simpler space. "Ultimately, what's most terrifying is not the place, but that Charles Wallace is not Charles Wallace—his mind has been consumed by the IT," says Shohan. The brain room was inspired, however, by various representations of dark matter and microscopic organic shapes, all in keeping with the scientific bent of L'Engle's novel.

While ultimately Meg must fight the battle alone, every visual detail supports her effort to overcome the IT.

Dr. Alex Murry looking for a way out

Concept artwork of Camazotz that proves even solid ground isn't so solid on this planet

The group faces unknown dangers on the dark planet of Camazotz

Calvin, Charles Wallace, and Meg have a strange experience eating in another world

Charles Wallace undergoes a terrifying transformation on Camazotz

Dr. Alex Murry tries to connect with his son on Camazotz

Charles Wallace taken over by the IT

Reese Witherspoon as Mrs. Whatsit and Deric McCabe as Charles Wallace share a moment on set

Calvin O'Keefe and Meg Murry

Meg Murry and Calvin O'Keefe

Concept artwork of the planet Ixchel

CHAPTER NINE
THE WORLD OF IXCHEL

But with the tentacle came the same delicate fragrance that moved across her with the breeze, and she felt a soft, tingling warmth go all through her that momentarily assuaged her pain. She felt suddenly sleepy.

I must look as strange to it as it looks to me, she thought drowsily, and then realized with a shock that of course the beast couldn't see her at all. Nevertheless a reassuring sense of safety flowed through her with the warmth which continued to seep deep into her as the beast touched her. Then it picked her up, cradling her in two of its four arms.

—Madeleine L'Engle, *A Wrinkle in Time*

The planet of Ixchel is a place of healing and relief for Meg. Her father and her brother are safe, but she has been wounded. In a safe and loving hideaway, she will recover her strength and then travel back to Earth. Meg is at peace here, as she was on Uriel, but Ixchel is not a place of overflowing beauty. It is still and calm and inspiring.

Although Meg's emotions on Ixchel are warm, production designer Naomi Shohan focused on cool, clear colors in this portion of the movie. "I just immediately saw this planet as glowing and beautiful," she says, "but in a northern lights sort of way, with everything in a particular shade of blue, like glacial water." Paco Delgado's costumes followed a similar color scheme. Within this soothing landscape, the art department needed to visualize Aunt Beast, the faceless character who nurses Meg back to health with unconditional love. "What is the essence of Aunt Beast?" Shohan asked herself. "She's the ultimate hug." Her team of artists concluded that the best way to show this feeling would be to envelop Meg in something warm. "Aunt Beast is sort of like a beanbag," says Shohan. "All comfort and love."

Of course it would be difficult to film a walking beanbag, so Aunt Beast would be

Concept artwork of the giant creature that Meg comes to call Aunt Beast

designed in post-production. The rest of the scene was filmed on a soundstage, and Mark Hawker was tasked with creating something that would stand in for Aunt Beast until the computer-generated imagery (CGI) was complete. "We'd make Aunt Beast in CGI later," Hawker says, "but we had to film Meg now. Finally, we rigged up something like a pita pocket—a hairy pita pocket—and put her inside it. Some guys in blue suits held it up, cradling Meg, so we could get the shots."

"What is the essence of Aunt Beast? She's the ultimate hug."

—NAOMI SHOHAN, PRODUCTION DESIGNER

As Meg snuggles, Aunt Beast sings a soothing lullaby, which eventually triggers the tesser that brings Meg back to Earth. This is where the various strands of the story converge: Meg's personal journey as well as the journeys into philosophy and science. The great beauty of the song acts almost like the process of sonoluminescence, where sound is fed into water with such intensity that it briefly creates a star. Here, the powerful beauty of the song creates the way for Meg to travel back in space and time, rejoining her family at home just an instant after she left it in the first place.

Sketches and development of Aunt Beast and her kind on Ixchel

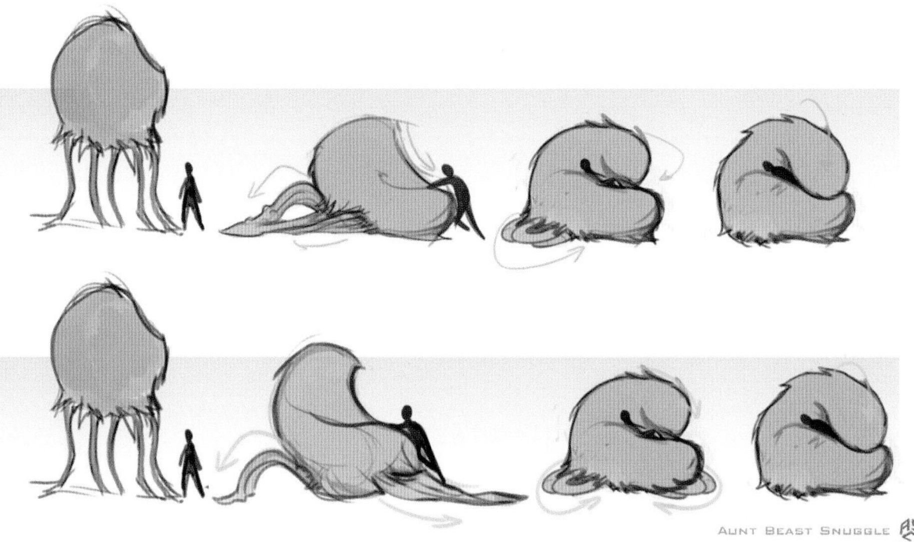

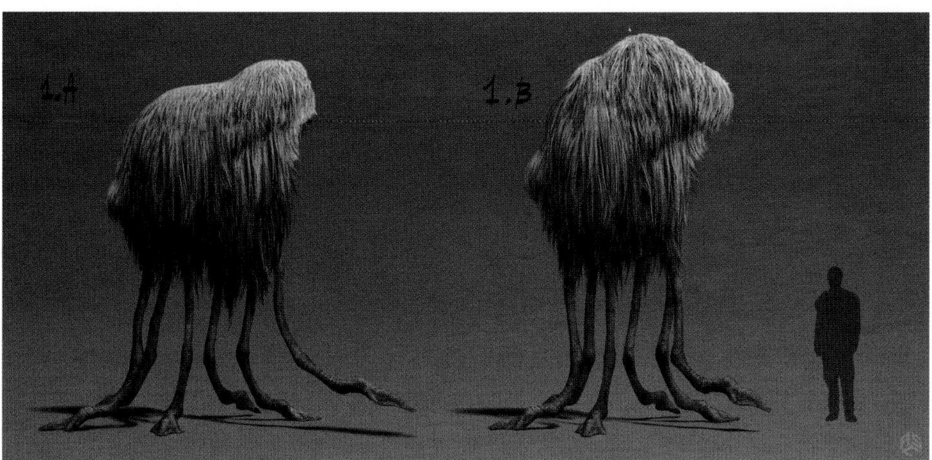

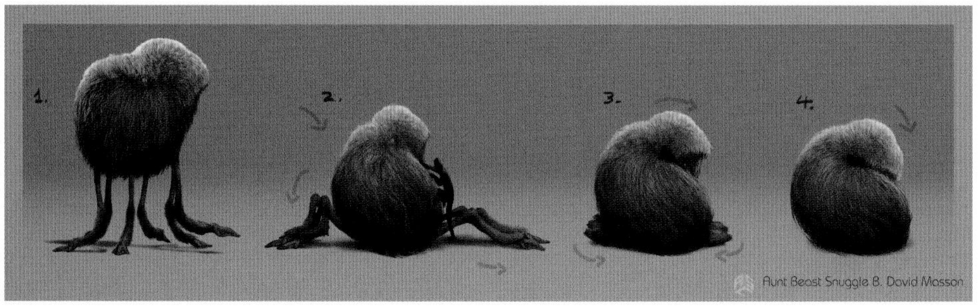

Concept artwork of Aunt Beast's dwelling place

The creatures of Ixchel walking with the three kids

Calvin looks on as Dr. Alex Murry and Charles Wallace reunite

TESSERING

Meg Murry explains the concept of tessering, the process by which travel across vast distances is made possible by taking advantage of warps—wrinkles—in gravitational fields

"You have to have certain inner qualities and a certain inner strength to tesser well. That's what Meg has to find on her journey. At the end of the film, you'll see what a great tesser is and you'll understand not just the scientific term, but what a tesseract really encompasses from the inside out. What it means to truly be one with the universe."

—AVA DuVERNAY, DIRECTOR

An important part of Meg's adventure is her process of finding inner strength, letting go of fear and self-doubt, and learning to tesser well

Dr. Alex Murry and his daughter share a moment

CHAPTER TEN
THE LEGACY OF *A WRINKLE IN TIME*

"You mean you're comparing our lives to a sonnet? A strict form, but freedom within it?"

"Yes," Mrs Whatsit said. "You're given the form but you have to write the sonnet yourself. What you say is completely up to you."

"Please," Meg said. "Please. If I've got to go I want to go."

—Madeleine L'Engle, *A Wrinkle in Time*

As Madeleine L'Engle's granddaughter, Charlotte Jones Voiklis has spent a lifetime with the author's legacy. While she is eager to protect it, she also knows how L'Engle herself felt about her work. "I don't remember the first time I read the book . . . It has always been a part of my earliest memories," says Jones Voiklis. "But I do remember being aware that many other people loved the book. One of the many things my grandmother always said about her work—and she wrote more than sixty books—was that the books didn't belong to just her. Once an artist puts something out in the world it belongs to everybody, and she took that very seriously."

Director Ava DuVernay carries that mantle solemnly, with determination to make the beloved book feel new again. She explains, "The reason why generations of people have gravitated toward this book is because it has an edge. It was on the edge

> "Every scene in this story has a little gem inside. I am so excited to unwrap all these little treasures when I get to set each day."
> —AVA DUVERNAY, DIRECTOR

of imagination and adventure in 1963, and now when we're talking about ways to make the story inclusive and be at the forefront of imagery and storytelling in 2018." She strives to reach two audiences: those whose imaginations lit up with a story they loved, and those whose imaginations are still open to its wonder.

Cast and crew alike are in awe of DuVernay's achievement. Screenwriter Jennifer Lee praises the director's broad interests and keen vision, saying,

Ava DuVernay directs the cameraman

Calvin and Meg

"Working with Ava has been extraordinary. She's so brilliant and so collaborative. Ava and I will get together and we'll start a conversation about bullies when we were kids, and what that felt like, and then by the end of the conversation we're trying to disprove Einstein's theory of relativity. . . . She'll go anywhere, she goes deep, and she wants to create something that will evoke the book but give people something they've never seen before."

And in these unsettled times, *A Wrinkle in Time* is not just a part of the conversation, but a potential guide toward the future. Producer Catherine Hand remembers the book's early days. "I read the book around the time of the Kennedy assassination and I remember adults around me saying that hope had died, which was a hard thing for a young girl to hear. The book gave me a sense of hope and courage and helped me

Meg, Charles Wallace, and Calvin on Camazotz

"One of the many things my grandmother always said about her work . . . was that the books didn't belong to just her. Once an artist puts something out in the world it belongs to everybody, and she took that very seriously."
—CHARLOTTE JONES VOIKLIS, MADELEINE L'ENGLE'S GRANDAUGHTER

to understand that while evil does exist, it can be overcome, which is why the perfect time for this movie to be released is right now."

As a story about time travel, *A Wrinkle in Time* is truly timeless, and it contains a valuable road map toward a future time, as well. "One of the most inspiring things about the story," says Hand, "is that it speaks to the human potential for good and for love. To Madeleine, love is action: how we treat one another with our actions, not just our words."

The film puts the timeless message even more simply: "Be a warrior."

Wherever you are in the universe.

Principal Jenkins

Veronica Kiley at school

Calvin O'Keefe discovering that not all is as it seems in the farthest reaches of the universe

Meg Murry and Dr. Alex Murry

"This is where we leave you, to
be our warriors for Earth."
—MRS. WHICH

ACKNOWLEDGMENTS

With abundant thank yous to the amazing team at FSG: Joy Peskin, Janine O'Malley, and most particularly Melissa Warten,who has patience to spare. Thanks also to Lauren Burniac, who opened doors that had seemed closed, and to Catherine Hand, Mark Hawker, Alison Taylor, Paco Delgado, and Naomi Shohan, who gave so generously of their time. Caitlin Dodson and Dale Kennedy connected me to invaluable information to make this book possible. I am so grateful to the director, the production team, the cast and crew of this film for sharing their thoughts and experiences. And to Madeleine L'Engle, for writing books that have sustained me since childhood.

—K.E.